iking 6.95 403

S0-BFA-346

iking 6.95 403

MT. ST. BERNARD COLLEGE
HERBERTON N.Q. 4872

14707

MT. ST. BERNARD
152·4
HERBERTON
SAN
COLLEGE

LET'S DISCUSS

LOVE, HATE AND OTHER FEELINGS

Pete Sanders and Steve Myers

Franklin Watts
LONDON · SYDNEY

Contents

© Aladdin Books Ltd 1996

All rights reserved

Designed and produced by
Aladdin Books Ltd
28 Percy Street
London W1P 0LD

First published in
Great Britain in 1996 by
Franklin Watts
96 Leonard Street
London EC2A 4RH

ISBN: 0 7496 2458 2

A catalogue record for this
book is available from the
British Library.

Printed in Belgium

Designer   Tessa Barwick
Editor   Alex Edmonds
Illustrator   Mike Lacey
Picture   Brooks
Research   Krikler
              Research

Pete Sanders is Senior
Lecturer in health education
at the University of North
London. He was a head
teacher for ten years and has
written many books on social
issues for children.

Steve Myers is a freelance
writer who has co-written
other titles in this series and
worked on several
educational projects for
children.

The consultant, Julia Cole, is
counsellor and psychosexual
therapist for Relate. She is
press officer for National
Relate, and agony aunt for
Essentials magazine.

HOW TO USE THIS BOOK

The books in this series are intended to help young people to understand more about personal issues that may affect their lives. Each book can be read by a child alone, or together with a parent, teacher or helper, so that there is an opportunity to talk through ideas as they come up. Issues raised in the storyline are explored in the accompanying text, inviting further discussion.

At the end of the book there is a section called "What Can We Do?" This section provides practical ideas which will be useful for both young people and adults, as well as a list of the names and addresses of organisations and helplines, providing further information and support.

—1— Introduction

Feelings are a powerful force in our lives. Total health is not just about physical fitness. As you grow up it is just as important to look after your emotional well-being also.

Learning to understand and express positive and negative emotions appropriately is a vital part of life. This book discusses why you have feelings and how they can affect you, and suggests ways of handling them correctly. Each chapter introduces a different aspect of the subject, illustrated by a continuing storyline. The characters in the story deal with situations which many young people experience. By the end you will have learned more about a variety of feelings, and the effects they can have on your life. You will also understand the best ways of expressing them, and know how to deal with difficult emotions.

— 2 — Emotions

Everybody is capable of a whole range of feelings. Love and hate are probably the two most intense emotions you can feel.

Feelings are part of what gives life variety and interest. If you could not respond emotionally, you would be just like a robot! You don't just experience the different kinds of feelings, but also different intensities of those feelings. Making sense of emotions is not always easy, and can be especially difficult at certain times of your life, such as during puberty.

Sometimes feelings can be unpredictable. The strength or suddenness of an emotion may then take you by surprise.

The true nature of emotions is not yet fully understood. Scientists know that when you experience a feeling, physical changes occur in the body. Hormones, the chemicals which control much of what happens in your body, play a large part in this. When you are nervous or frightened you might tremble or have sweaty palms. If you're embarrassed you may go red as blood rushes to the skin's surface. Or you may not always be aware of the change. Knowing how to handle your feelings is important. This involves learning to understand why you have particular feelings, and how and when to express them properly.

▽ Liam Walker and his friends were discussing the exam they were about to sit.

▽ Just round the corner, Dionne Benson was also worried.

△ Patti was Dionne's sister. The two of them didn't get on very well.

△ Salim interrupted them, with a nasty surprise.

▽ After the exam, everybody was discussing how it went.

△ Dionne still didn't feel optimistic about her results.

▽ Liam and Salim walked home together.

▽ Liam also had to get home. It was his brother Colin's birthday.

△ Their father had been killed in a car accident two years ago.

△ Their gran always seemed to treat them like they were both still five years old.

DIONNE DOESN'T LIKE SPIDERS EVEN THOUGH SHE KNOWS THERE IS NOTHING TO BE AFRAID OF.

Many emotions are the result of things that have happened to you in similar situations. If you have been unfairly treated by someone you might feel unable to trust that person. Or, if you were frightened by a dog as a young child, you may associate all dogs with the fear you once felt. Sometimes it is not obvious where a particular emotional response comes from. Trying to understand the reason why you are feeling a certain way can help you to handle the emotion.

THE REACTIONS OF OTHER PEOPLE ALSO PLAY A PART IN DECIDING HOW YOU FEEL.

Small children might initially be scared of clowns. But the positive responses of others help them realise that there is nothing to worry about. People often expect you to feel a certain way, the same way they feel. However, emotional reactions are personal and aren't necessarily the same as those of others.

COLIN DOESN'T KNOW WHY HE'S DEPRESSED ON HIS BIRTHDAY.

Feelings can't be turned on and off at will. Sometimes you may have intense emotions, without knowing why. You could wake up feeling sad or irritable, yet not be able to think of anything which can account for how you feel. Although this can be annoying and confusing, it is perfectly natural.

—3— Expressing Feelings

"I won a prize at school. It was so unexpected and I was so happy, I just burst into tears! It was strange – I don't know where the feeling came from!"

The way in which somebody responds emotionally will depend on the feeling itself, the intensity of it, and the situation he or she is in. Someone's cultural and social background may also influence the way feelings are shown and managed, both in public and privately. Some people are outgoing and express their feelings easily. Others find it much harder.

Bottling up your feelings can often make a situation much worse.

There are many ways of showing emotion, for instance, smiling, laughing, shouting, crying, even fighting. Many people make their feelings obvious – they may throw their arms around to stress the point they are making, or might hug, kiss or touch people they know, to show affection. Others can have the same feelings, but express them quietly, and in a less obvious way. In some situations, you may need to be diplomatic and not describe your feelings fully, to spare someone else's. Sometimes, you will have feelings you don't like, or are not proud of. All feelings are okay to have, but not all are acceptable to act on. Learning to recognise and accept your emotions, and to respond appropriately can take time, but is an important part of growing up.

SOME PEOPLE THINK CERTAIN EXPRESSIONS OF EMOTION ARE UNACCEPTABLE.

For instance, you may have heard it said that it's okay for girls to cry, but not boys. This is not true. In fact, your gender makes no difference either to the feelings you have or to the way you might want to express them.

DIONNE FINDS IT HARD TO EXPLAIN TO HER PARENTS HER REAL FEELINGS.

People do not always express their real emotions. This is often the case with feelings such as love, anger or grief. People may disguise emotions, perhaps by appearing unconcerned or light-hearted. Or they might be moody. Sometimes they may try to take out their feelings on someone, by being nasty, or accusing them of causing the problem.

**CASE STUDY:
FARIBA, AGED 13**

"I feel really guilty, because I've upset my gran. She visited us last month and gave me a gift – a brooch, which I thought was a bit old-fashioned. I did say thank you, but I was getting ready to go out with friends, and I didn't make a fuss. Mum told me later that my gran was really hurt by the way I treated her. The brooch belonged to my great grandmother, and it meant a lot to my gran to be giving it to me. It wouldn't have hurt me to have spent a few minutes talking to her, and shown an interest. I'd still have been in time to meet my friends. I didn't mean to take her for granted. If I'd only bothered to thank her properly I could have saved all this upset, and I wouldn't have hurt her feelings."

−4− Feeling Good

"I enjoy looking forward to things like holidays. I imagine all the things I'll do. To me it's almost as good as the holiday itself!"

Most of us like to feel good, and think that this is what creates a happy life. Your outlook and the way you feel about yourself can play a major part in deciding how you feel. Many people believe that a positive outlook and a sense of your own self-worth are vital in helping you to feel happy and to form strong, healthy relationships with other people. There are all kinds of positive feelings – joy, wonder, happiness, excitement, satisfaction and, of course, love.

Other people can often help you to feel good about yourself. Many people get pleasure from sharing special experiences and times with others.

Loving relationships are very important to most people's lives. You can feel different types and levels of love for a variety of people. The love you feel for your family may not be the same as that you have for friends. Mature love involves trust and honest, open communication. As you grow up, your feelings may change, and this can be confusing. Nobody feels good all the time. Everybody will experience emotional ups and downs in life. Feeling good involves wanting the best for other people as well as yourself. Your own happiness should never be at the expense of someone else's.

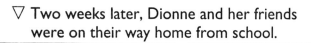

▽ Two weeks later, Dionne and her friends were on their way home from school.

BETH, WHAT WAS WRONG WITH YOU TODAY? YOU'RE USUALLY SO GOOD AT MATHS, BUT YOU GOT NEARLY EVERY ANSWER WRONG.

I COULDN'T CONCENTRATE.

WE ALL KNOW WHAT YOU WERE THINKING ABOUT - YOUR DREAM GUY, PASCAL.

YOU NEVER STOP TALKING ABOUT HIM. IT'S PATHETIC.

I DON'T CARE. I LIKE HIM - THOUGH I DON'T THINK HE LIKES ME VERY MUCH. HE SEEMS EMBARRASSED AROUND ME.

MAYBE YOU'RE TRYING TOO HARD. WHEN I WAS AT YOUR PLACE AT THE WEEKEND, YOU HARDLY SPOKE A WORD TO ME. YOU JUST FOLLOWED MR WONDERFUL AROUND!

▽ Liam and Salim left the others. Liam asked about Salim's mum.

SHE'S GETTING MUCH BETTER. LAST SATURDAY WE ALL DROVE TO THE COAST FOR THE DAY. IT WAS REALLY GOOD FUN, ALL BEING OUT TOGETHER.

DIONNE BENSON? ACTUALLY, I QUITE LIKE HER. SHE'S GOOD FUN - THOUGH I'M GLAD HER PARENTS AREN'T MINE. WHY? DO YOU FANCY HER OR SOMETHING?

LEAVE IT OUT. NO, I WAS JUST THINKING I MIGHT ASK HER TO THE CINEMA WITH ME.

CAN I ASK YOU SOMETHING? IT'S A BIT EMBARRASSING. WHAT DO YOU THINK OF DIONNE?

△ Liam liked Dionne a lot. But he felt very shy about saying anything to her.

▽ At home that evening, Liam spoke to Colin about how he felt.

DID YOU HAVE A GIRLFRIEND WHEN YOU WERE MY AGE?

THERE'S THIS GIRL AT SCHOOL. I WANTED TO ASK HER OUT, BUT I DON'T KNOW HOW. I WISH DAD WERE HERE. I DON'T FEEL LIKE I CAN TALK TO MUM ABOUT STUFF LIKE THAT.

NO, NOT REALLY. BUT THERE WAS LOTS OF TALK ABOUT WHO FANCIED WHO AND THAT KIND OF THING. WHY?

MUM'S OKAY. MIND YOU, DAD WAS GREAT AT UNDERSTANDING EXACTLY HOW I FELT.

△ Colin suggested that Liam ask Dionne to the end of term dance at school.

BETH HAS A CRUSH ON PASCAL.

Crushes – periods of intense emotional or sexual attraction to someone – can be very confusing. Many people experience them as they grow up. You can have a crush on a person you know, or a pop or TV star. Some have crushes on someone of the same sex. This does not mean they are lesbian or gay.

IT'S IMPORTANT TO KEEP THINGS IN PERSPECTIVE.

Beth's infatuation with Pascal is stopping her from concentrating on schoolwork. Both positive and negative emotions can be strong. Feeling incredibly happy all the time could be as stressful as being angry or depressed.

FACTFILE:
FEELING GOOD

Most positive feelings are not a problem but there are some things to keep in mind:

- People can be carried away by extreme good feelings. This may make them absent-minded or careless.
- Don't let feelings for someone cloud your judgement. Some young people are persuaded into situations they regret.
- Many young people have tried alcohol or drugs, believing they will give them a pleasurable feeling. In fact, the negative effect on their lives can be devastating.
- Remember that not everyone will be feeling as good as you are! Don't forget other people's feelings too.

−5− Feeling Bad

Just as optimism – a positive out-look – can help you feel good, pessimism – a negative outlook – can have the opposite effect.

Many life events and changes are stressful. Nobody can avoid certain times when you will experience and have to cope with strong negative feelings. There are all kinds of emotions which can make you feel bad. These often seem to feel more intense than positive ones, and may sometimes be the ones we remember most. Hatred is a destructive feeling. Most of those who say they hate someone actually mean they dislike the person. Sometimes prejudice and discrimination create hatred.

Many people deal with anger by exploding at the slightest irritation. Others are easy-going, and rarely lose their temper. Anger is very different from aggression and can be positive, if it is used in the correct way, to express strong feelings about a situation.

Guilt is a very difficult emotion that you may feel if you've acted wrongly. Sometimes people can play on these feelings by trying to make you feel guilty about something, to get you to do something that they want. It is good to be able to realise when this is happening to you, and challenge it.

Anxiety is very hard to handle. If it becomes too intense it may blot out everything else. Worry about an exam, or important occasion can turn into anxiety, which becomes just like an obsession, and takes over your life.

We all have disagreements. But arguments where people just shout at each other, won't help to solve the problem.

▽ A week later, Liam came home to find his mum crying.

> SOMETIMES IT'S GOOD TO CRY, LIAM. IT STOPS ME FROM BOTTLING UP MY FEELINGS. I MISS YOUR DAD VERY MUCH, AND IT'S HARD SOMETIMES TO THINK THAT WE'LL NEVER SEE HIM AGAIN.

> MUM, DON'T CRY. I HATE TO SEE YOU SAD ABOUT DAD.

> IT'S OKAY. I WAS JUST WRITING THE MEMORIAL TO GO IN THE PAPER NEXT WEEK. IT MADE ME REMEMBER SOME OF THE THINGS HE USED TO SAY.

> IT'S NOT FAIR. DAD WOULD STILL BE HERE NOW IF IT WASN'T FOR THAT MAN DRIVING TOO FAST. I HATE HIM. HE SHOULD BE THE ONE THAT DIED.

△ Liam's father had been knocked down by a speeding driver.

> I KNOW YOU LOVED YOUR DAD, AND HOW UNFAIR YOU THINK IT IS. BUT IT WAS AN ACCIDENT. THAT MAN WAS UPSET TOO. HE DIDN'T MEAN TO DO IT. HATING HIM WON'T HELP ANY OF US, LIAM.

▽ Two days later, Beth called round for Dionne on the way to school. She and her dad were arguing.

> I DON'T UNDERSTAND YOU, DIONNE. YOU DON'T SEEM TO WANT TO DO WELL ANY MORE.

> MAYBE YOU NEED TO WORK HARDER.

> YEAH, AND MAYBE YOU NEED TO MIND YOUR OWN BUSINESS. I'M OFF, OR I'LL BE LATE FOR SCHOOL. AND WE CAN'T HAVE THAT, CAN WE?

△ Liam knew his mum was right, but he felt so angry about everything.

> CALM DOWN! WHAT WAS THAT ALL ABOUT?

> WHAT DO YOU THINK? ALL THEY DO IS COMPARE ME TO PATTI. I CAN NEVER BE GOOD ENOUGH AT ANYTHING. I'M NOT PATTI. THEY DON'T UNDERSTAND.

> I WAS JUST WONDERING IF...I MEAN IF YOU MIGHT...I MEAN MAYBE YOU'D LIKE TO... DIONNE WOULD YOU GO TO THE DISCO WITH ME?

> OH! SURE...OK. DON'T WORRY. MAYBE SOME OTHER TIME. LOOK, I'D BETTER GO IN. SEE YOU AROUND, DIONNE.

▷ As they arrived at school, Liam asked to speak to Dionne alone.

> THANKS, LIAM, BUT I CAN'T. I'M GOING WITH SALIM.

△ Liam rushed away, feeling foolish. Salim had some explaining to do.

FACTFILE:
FEELING BAD

FACTFILE:
FEELING BAD

Here are some points to remember about handling negative feelings:

- The intensity of emotions often changes or becomes easier to deal with over time, though they may initially seem overwhelming.
- Talking to someone you trust about your feelings can help, as can focusing on positive feelings.
- Try not to act on bad feelings immediately. Give yourself time to think, and work out how you feel.
- Often it can be tempting to let out feelings like anger at just whoever is there, whether or not they deserve it! Make sure your emotions are properly directed.

MRS WALKER KNOWS THAT CRYING CAN HELP HER WORK THROUGH HER GRIEF.

At times, getting angry or crying can help to release emotions which you can't otherwise express. Grief is a mix of thoughts, memories and emotions. It can be one of the most difficult feelings to deal with. Facing these feelings is the only way of coming to terms with them.

LIAM SAYS HE HATES THE DRIVER OF THE CAR AND BLAMES HIM FOR HIS FATHER'S DEATH.

His mum knows that feelings like this do not do anybody any good. Hatred and jealousy can stop you from getting on with your own life and put a strain on all your relationships. They affect how you feel about things, including yourself, and can make you lose your self-esteem.

–6– Feelings Towards Others

"I felt awful when my best friend moved away. We knew each other so well, one could always tell how the other felt. I was so sad."

Whether you prefer the company of a few close friends, or enjoy being around a lot of people, you will always come into contact with others. As you go through life, you will develop a variety of different relationships. Some may last a long time. Others will not. The feelings that you develop for other people can be some of the strongest you will ever experience.

Being in a group can be fun, but it is sometimes difficult to get your point across.

Many people are very close to the members of their family. But this isn't always the case. You can't choose who makes up your family. For this reason, some people feel closer to the friends they make. Good communication is a vital part of all relationships if they are to work properly.

Trust is another important factor. Relationships in which people are not being honest with each other are unlikely to be satisfactory. Sometimes, people may try to make you do something you don't want to, or which you know is wrong. They might play on your feelings, saying things like 'you would if you were really my friend'. Or they might dare you. These tactics are very unfair and a true friend will not use them.

Remember that everybody makes mistakes occasionally. Part of being in a relationship may involve making allowances and not bearing grudges. You would hope that someone else would forgive you if you upset that person. In the same way, you may be asked to overlook other people's mistakes. People sometimes are jealous of someone else's success. Jealousy harms relationships, and the way you feel about yourself. We should be able to enjoy other people's good fortune and be happy for them.

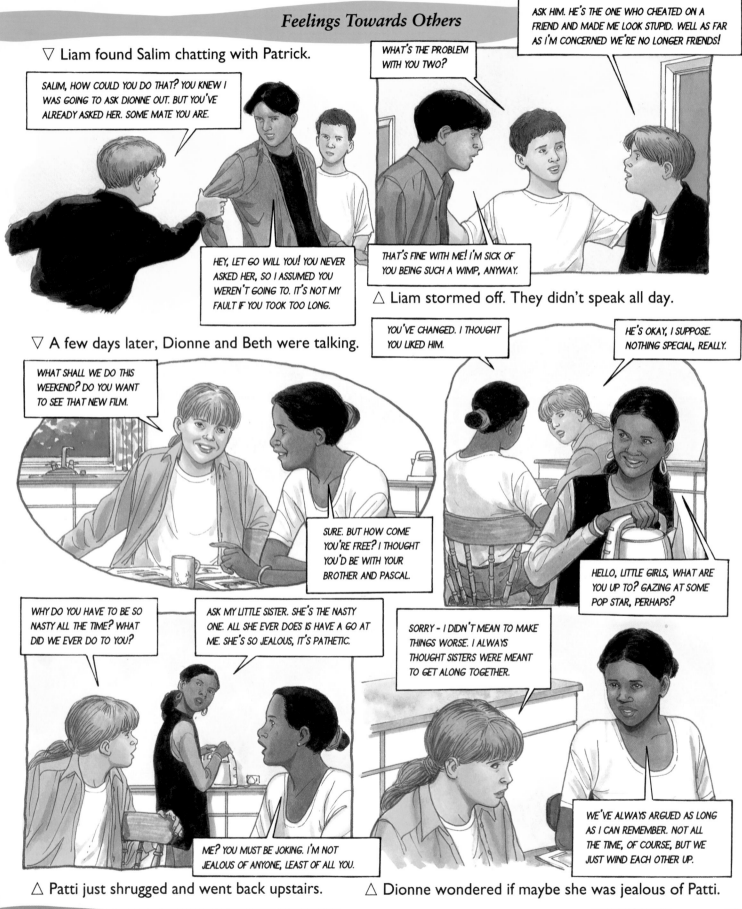

▽ Liam found Salim chatting with Patrick.

SALIM, HOW COULD YOU DO THAT? YOU KNEW I WAS GOING TO ASK DIONNE OUT. BUT YOU'VE ALREADY ASKED HER. SOME MATE YOU ARE.

HEY, LET GO WILL YOU! YOU NEVER ASKED HER, SO I ASSUMED YOU WEREN'T GOING TO. IT'S NOT MY FAULT IF YOU TOOK TOO LONG.

WHAT'S THE PROBLEM WITH YOU TWO?

ASK HIM. HE'S THE ONE WHO CHEATED ON A FRIEND AND MADE ME LOOK STUPID. WELL AS FAR AS I'M CONCERNED WE'RE NO LONGER FRIENDS!

THAT'S FINE WITH ME! I'M SICK OF YOU BEING SUCH A WIMP, ANYWAY.

△ Liam stormed off. They didn't speak all day.

▽ A few days later, Dionne and Beth were talking.

WHAT SHALL WE DO THIS WEEKEND? DO YOU WANT TO SEE THAT NEW FILM.

YOU'VE CHANGED. I THOUGHT YOU LIKED HIM.

HE'S OKAY, I SUPPOSE. NOTHING SPECIAL, REALLY.

SURE. BUT HOW COME YOU'RE FREE? I THOUGHT YOU'D BE WITH YOUR BROTHER AND PASCAL.

HELLO, LITTLE GIRLS, WHAT ARE YOU UP TO? GAZING AT SOME POP STAR, PERHAPS?

WHY DO YOU HAVE TO BE SO NASTY ALL THE TIME? WHAT DID WE EVER DO TO YOU?

ASK MY LITTLE SISTER. SHE'S THE NASTY ONE. ALL SHE EVER DOES IS HAVE A GO AT ME. SHE'S SO JEALOUS, IT'S PATHETIC.

SORRY - I DIDN'T MEAN TO MAKE THINGS WORSE. I ALWAYS THOUGHT SISTERS WERE MEANT TO GET ALONG TOGETHER.

ME? YOU MUST BE JOKING. I'M NOT JEALOUS OF ANYONE, LEAST OF ALL YOU.

WE'VE ALWAYS ARGUED AS LONG AS I CAN REMEMBER. NOT ALL THE TIME, OF COURSE, BUT WE JUST WIND EACH OTHER UP.

△ Patti just shrugged and went back upstairs.

△ Dionne wondered if maybe she was jealous of Patti.

CASE STUDY:
MARIA, AGED 15

"I really fancied this boy at school. But I didn't dare say anything to him, because I was sure he'd laugh at me. I had glasses, and braces on my teeth. I felt unattractive. I tried to think of ways to talk to him. Eventually I asked him to the school dance. He said yes, and afterwards told me he'd liked me for ages, but he'd been afraid to say anything too. We went to the dance and have been out a few times since then."

LIAM AND SALIM HAVE FALLEN OUT AND NO LONGER CONSIDER THEMSELVES FRIENDS.

Not all relationships stay the same. As you grow up, the nature of some may change. During puberty, many young people become more aware of the opposite sex, and may be attracted to someone. This feeling can be very strong and confusing at first. You might feel you are in love with the other person. However the strength of these first feelings will probably change and this is normal.

SOMETIMES, TRYING TO TELL SOMEONE HOW WE TRULY FEEL CAN MAKE US EMBARRASSED OR SHY.

Everyone likes to receive praise. Even so, many people feel uncomfortable with compliments or expressions of affection. Often embarrassment is caused not by how other people react, but how you think they will react. It can take a lot of strength to overcome this self-doubt, but it can be done. If you feel very shy in social situations, don't worry, just take things a step at a time. Most people find it gets easier with practice.

−7− *Handling Conflict*

"I realised our friendship was more important than winning an argument. In the end we agreed to disagree."

Conflicts are a normal part of life. If we all agreed with each other all the time, there would be no variety in life – it would be pretty boring. A brief squabble can be healthier than building up suspicion and resentment. However, when you are in conflict, your emotions may be very intense and sometimes people allow them to get in the way of finding a solution.

Keeping calm can be difficult, but it often stops many disagreements getting out of hand and helps in reaching a more effective solution.

Although you may feel very strongly about the issues involved, it's important to respect other people's right to express their opinion. Often the reason for a disagreement getting out of control is that those involved don't listen to each other properly, or jump in without thinking about what has been said. An effective way to solve most conflicts is to try to find an outcome which will satisfy all those concerned. This also means being prepared to have your own position challenged, and admitting when you are in the wrong.

Emotions like disappointment, hurt, anger and betrayal can feel overwhelming at first. Being caught up in such feelings may make it impossible to make sensible decisions and comments, and you might end up regretting what you do or say.

▽ Three weeks later Liam and Salim still weren't talking.

IT'S SATURDAY, LIAM. I THOUGHT YOU'D BE ROUND AT SALIM'S. DON'T TELL ME YOU TWO STILL AREN'T TALKING.

NOT UNTIL HE APOLOGISES.

WELL SINCE YOU WON'T TELL ME WHAT YOU ARGUED ABOUT IN THE FIRST PLACE, I CAN'T COMMENT. BUT YOU TWO WERE BEST FRIENDS, AND BOTH OF YOU HAVE TO WORK THIS OUT.

I DON'T SEE WHY I SHOULD TALK TO HIM.

MY OTHER FRIENDS HAVE SIDED WITH HIM, TOO. I HARDLY SEE ANYONE ANY MORE. IT'S NOT FAIR.

△ Liam was feeling lonely and confused. He couldn't see any way out of the situation.

▽ Meanwhile, Dionne had gone up to Patti's room to try and talk to her.

IF YOU'VE COME TO WRECK MY WORK AGAIN, YOU NEEDN'T BOTHER. I'VE SAVED EVERYTHING.

IT'S NOTHING LIKE THAT. PATTI, CAN WE TALK FOR A MINUTE? I'VE BEEN THINKING A LOT ABOUT WHAT YOU SAID BEFORE – ABOUT ME BEING JEALOUS OF YOU.

CAN WE DISCUSS IT LATER? I'M NOT IN THE MOOD FOR THIS RIGHT NOW.

IT'S IMPORTANT, PATTI. WE NEED TO TALK. WE CAN'T JUST KEEP ARGUING ALL THE TIME. OH, FORGET IT!

△ Patti ignored her. Dionne went downstairs, feeling upset.

▽ Later on, Dionne met Beth in town.

WHAT'S WRONG WITH YOU? YOU HAVEN'T SAID A WORD FOR AGES.

OH, LEAVE ME ALONE, CAN'T YOU? LOOK, I'M SORRY, BETH. I DIDN'T MEAN TO SNAP AT YOU. I'M IN A FOUL MOOD. I DON'T REALLY KNOW HOW I FEEL AT THE MOMENT.

LIAM AND SALIM ARE NOT LOOKING FOR A SOLUTION TO THE PROBLEM.
All relationships involve give and take. It's important to remember that other people's feelings matter too. At times you may need to experience disappointment or unhappiness so that somebody else can be happy. This should be by choice, but often, putting another person's well being above your own can make you feel good.

FACTFILE:
HANDLING DIFFERENCES

• Look at the reason for the conflict – is it worth falling out about?

• Think first, before you say anything.

• Try not just to swap insults – it won't solve anything and may make matters worse.

• Keep calm if you can. Shouting makes a lot of noise but very little progress.

• Don't bring up old disputes. Just concentrate on the main problem.

• Say how you feel, don't just make accusations. Look for ways of satisfying everyone involved.

• Remember you may not be right! Admitting you're wrong isn't easy. But, not doing so can prolong the conflict and just make you feel worse in the long run.

DIONNE SNAPPED AT BETH BECAUSE SHE'S FEELING MOODY.
A mood can affect how you respond in a particular situation. If you are in a bad mood, you might react emotionally to something which you would otherwise ignore. During puberty, mood swings – going from one set of feelings to another in a short time – are common.

–8– Coping With Difficult Feelings

"I thought the feeling would go away if I ignored it, but it didn't. In fact it began to get worse, until it was all I thought about."

It is very important to learn how and when to express your feelings appropriately. Most of the time you probably have no trouble handling them. From time to time, however, you will be in different situations which bring up strong or difficult emotions, which you will need to cope with. The first step is to recognise that you have a particular feeling. Just realising that you feel angry or jealous or sad will help to give you the understanding which you will need for coping with that feeling.

This may sound obvious, but some people try to cope by denying their emotions – pretending that they aren't happening. This will not help the situation. Others have turned to alcohol or drugs in order, they believe, to hide from, and forget, difficult feelings. In fact, instead of being an escape, drink and drugs can make feelings much worse, and have other detrimental effects on a person's life.

As you grow older, you will develop your own ways of coping. Not all feelings last for the same time, and dealing with an emotion doesn't always mean that it will disappear. For instance, grief may stay with someone forever, but will usually become less intense and easier to handle with time.

There are many different things that may help you deal with difficult feelings, such as listening to music, crying, going for a walk, or socialising with friends.

Coping With Difficult Feelings

▽ The end of term was approaching. Dionne had another test coming up, and wanted to do well.

NEED ANY HELP WITH YOUR REVISION?

NO THANKS, DAD. I'M FINE. IT'S ENGLISH THIS TIME. IT'S MY FAVOURITE SUBJECT. I'M SURE I'LL BE OKAY. IT'S SCIENCE I HAVE A PROBLEM WITH.

MAYBE YOU'RE NOT GIVING THE SUBJECT A CHANCE. IT'S IMPORTANT FOR YOUR FUTURE.

I DO GIVE IT A CHANCE. I JUST DON'T FIND IT INTERESTING. I DON'T EVEN KNOW WHAT I WANT TO BE WHEN I GROW UP,

I DON'T WANT TO LET YOU DOWN, BUT I FEEL AS THOUGH EVERYONE'S ON AT ME ALL THE TIME. IT'S LIKE MY WHOLE FUTURE'S ALREADY BEEN DECIDED AND NOBODY'S BOTHERED TO ASK ABOUT WHAT I WANT.

▽ Her dad apologised for putting pressure on her.

WE JUST WANT THE BEST FOR YOU, DIONNE. YOU'RE GOING THROUGH A LOT OF CHANGES.

HALF THE TIME I'M NOT SURE HOW I FEEL ABOUT ANYTHING AT ALL. IT'S SO CONFUSING FOR ME. I DON'T WANT TO MAKE THE WRONG DECISION.

I USED TO THINK I DIDN'T GET ON WITH PATTI BECAUSE SHE WAS SUCH A SWAT. NOW I THINK I WAS REALLY JEALOUS OF HER, BECAUSE SHE WAS ALWAYS THE ONE WITH THE GOOD GRADES.

▷ They talked for a long time. Dionne felt good to be discussing things properly at last.

▽ A few days later, Salim was waiting for Dionne outside school.

HI, DIONNE, ARE WE STILL ON FOR THE DISCO NEXT WEEK.

SALIM, I'D BEEN MEANING TO TELL YOU BEFORE. I CAN'T GO TO THE DANCE WITH YOU. IT'S PATTI'S BIRTHDAY - THE WHOLE FAMILY'S GOING OUT FOR A MEAL. I'M REALLY SORRY.

▽ The next day, Liam caught up with Salim.

△ Salim explained. He said he'd felt disappointed when she told him.

△ The two of them laughed and went into class.

△ The following week, Dionne went into Patti's room to give her her present.

△ The two of them sat down at the computer and started to load the progamme.

DIONNE AND HER DAD HAVE CLEARED THE AIR BY TALKING ABOUT THEIR FEELINGS.

This is one of the most effective ways of dealing with difficult emotions or situations. Talking to someone you trust can help to clarify both how you are feeling and what the problem is. You might want to think about who you can discuss your own feelings with – not just the bad ones.

YOU CAN'T COPE WITH A FEELING IF YOU PRETEND YOU DON'T HAVE IT.

You need to be honest with yourself about your deepest feelings. Sometimes, if you can't discuss a situation with someone else, having a mental discussion about it can be a helpful tool to work through a sudden rush of emotion, and perhaps discover exactly how your are feeling.

LIAM AND SALIM ARE BOTH DISAPPOINTED THAT DIONNE IS NOT GOING TO THE DANCE.

Being let down by others is never easy. If someone rejects an offer of friendship, or betrays you, it is very upsetting. It's important, not to let the actions of other people affect your self-esteem. The urge to retaliate might be strong, but revenge may not be as satisfying as you think. Often it just makes the situation worse. Remembering how it feels to be let down ourselves can help to make sure we try not to disappoint people.

Feeling Good About Yourself

> "*People can only make you feel bad about yourself with your permission.*" Eleanor Roosevelt, wife of a former US President.

Some of the most important feelings are those you have about yourself. They can affect how you deal with and feel about others, and affect how you respond to different situations. Research has suggested that those people with good self-esteem – a strong belief in their own worth – are better able to handle social situations and to form successful relationships. Self-esteem does not just happen overnight. It is developed throughout your life, and may be influenced by many things, such as your friends and family and the experiences you have.

Most people want to be liked. In order for this to happen some think they need to act in a certain way, and pretend to be something they're not. Trying to change your character to impress someone won't help to form a good relationship. The first step in being liked is to be comfortable with who you are and to like yourself. This involves knowing that you're not 'better' or 'worse' than the next person. People have a variety of skills – some of your friends may be cleverer at a particular subject or able to do something you can't, but the reverse is also true. In the same way, self-esteem is not about boasting, or thinking you will always be in the right. It involves being able to listen to and accept criticism, provided it is reasonable.

Experiencing bad feelings sometimes helps us make the most of good feelings we have.

▽ It was the start of term.

I CAN'T BELIEVE THE HOLIDAYS ARE OVER ALREADY. WHO'S THIS?

THIS IS BARBARA. SHE'S JUST MOVED SCHOOLS. SHE STARTS HERE TODAY.

IT MUST BE DIFFICULT HAVING TO CHANGE SCHOOLS HALFWAY THROUGH THE YEAR.

IT IS A BIT. WE HAD TO MOVE TO THIS TOWN BECAUSE OF DAD'S JOB. I DON'T KNOW ANYONE HERE.

HI. I REALLY LIKE YOUR EARRINGS. WHERE DID YOU GET THEM FROM?

DON'T WORRY. YOU'LL SOON MAKE FRIENDS. WE'LL LOOK AFTER YOU.

OH AND YOU EXPECT THAT'LL MAKE HER FEEL OK?

▽ A month into the new term, there was due to be another science test.

THIS WAS A GREAT IDEA, DIONNE. THANKS FOR INVITING US ROUND. IT'S A REALLY USEFUL PROGRAM.

PATRICK SAYS YOU KEEP GOING ON ABOUT BARBARA. HE SAYS YOU FANCY HER.

THAT SHOWS HOW MUCH HE KNOWS. ANYWAY, SALIM AND I AREN'T GOING TO FALL OUT OVER SOMETHING LIKE THAT AGAIN.

IT'S GOOD ISN'T IT? BUT IT'S FUNNY THOUGH. IT'S MUCH EASIER NOW THAT I DON'T FEEL SO MUCH PRESSURE ON ME TO DO WELL.

YOU WERE REALLY PATHETIC OVER THE DISCO. I NEVER REALISED HOW MUCH TROUBLE I'D CAUSED.

▽ Beth said it wasn't Dionne's fault.

SHE'S RIGHT. WE NEVER EVEN STOPPED TO THINK ABOUT HOW YOU MIGHT FEEL.

SOMEHOW THAT DOESN'T MAKE IT ANY EASIER.

IT'S THINKING FOR YOURSELF AND IN THE END MAKING YOUR OWN DECISIONS. LIKE I'M NOT GOING TO COMPLETELY GIVE UP THE IDEA OF BEING A DOCTOR. AS DAD SAYS, I MIGHT STILL CHANGE MY MIND AND I MIGHT NOT. WHO KNOWS? BUT I'LL DECIDE.

IT'S SO EASY TO FORGET HOW THINGS CAN MAKE OTHER PEOPLE FEEL. SOMETIMES IT'S REALLY HARD TO KNOW WHAT YOU'RE SUPPOSED TO DO. IT GETS REALLY CONFUSING.

I GUESS IT'S THE SAME FOR EVERYONE.

WELL I KNOW ONE THING. YOU ALL MIGHT BE CONFIDENT ABOUT THIS TEST, BUT I NEED TO DO SOME MORE REVISION!

△ They all went back to work.

SELF-ESTEEM CAN BE AFFECTED BY MOOD, AND BY THE MESSAGES WE ARE GIVEN.

If you feel good, and someone pays you a compliment, you will usually accept it. If you are irritable or depressed, you might think you don't deserve it. Most people respond positively to praise. In the same way, if others say negative things about you often enough, you may begin to believe them. This is why it's important to have a strong belief in yourself, understand how moods can affect you, and be able to separate constructive criticism from unfair comments.

IT IS ALSO IMPORTANT TO RECOGNISE OTHER PEOPLE'S RIGHTS TO HAVE THEIR OWN VIEWS AND FEELINGS.

People are different. Respecting other people doesn't mean that you have to like everyone. Nor does it mean that you can't challenge opinions which you don't agree with, or which you believe are discriminating against others.

CASE STUDY: PATRICK, AGED 12

"One of the boys at school used to make fun of me and call me names. He said I was stupid and made nasty comments about my family. At first I tried to shrug them off, but he just kept on at me. He had a group of friends with him, and they just laughed at me. I became really depressed. I talked to my brother in the end, and he helped me see that this boy was just a bully. None of what he was saying was true. I realised that by showing that I was hurt by the comments, I was giving the bully power over me. I made up my mind not to let him get to me, and it seems to have worked."

What Can We Do?

"It really helps me to realise that all of these new feelings are normal, and that I'm not the only one who has them."

Life involves many different experiences. Learning how to accept the whole range of feelings they might bring up – good and bad – and deal with them appropriately, is a vital part of growing up. Having read this book you will know more about different kinds of emotions, the effects they can have on you and other people, and some of the ways you can express them properly.

Succesful communication can help you to understand or explain emotions, and sort out all kinds of problems – even the most complex!

You will understand how important it is to have an outlet for difficult feelings. You might want to think of ideas you can use to work through your feelings. Are there any situations which you find particularly problematic? Don't forget that just as you may want to talk to someone else about your own feelings, others may look to you to listen to their problems. Adults sometimes forget that young people may be experiencing some very strong emotions – perhaps for the first time – especially during puberty. They can help by understanding how confusing this can be for many people.

Adults and young people who have read this book together may like to discuss their feelings about the issues raised. Anyone who would like to talk to someone not directly involved about aspects of emotional well-being may be able to obtain information, support or advice from the organisations listed below.

YOUTH ACCESS
Magazine Business Centre
11 Newarke Street
Leicester
LE1 5SS
Tel: 0116 2558763

CHILDLINE
2nd Floor,
Royal Mail Building
Studd Street
London
N1 0QW
Tel: 0171 239 1000
Tel: 0800 1111
(24 hour helpline)

CHILDREN'S LEGAL CENTRE
University of Essex
Wivenhoe Park
Colchester
Essex
CO4 3SQ
Tel: 01206 873820

THE CHILDREN'S SOCIETY
Margery Street
London
WC1X 0JL
Tel: 0171 837 4299

THE NATIONAL ASSOCIATION OF CITIZENS' ADVICE BUREAUX
115 Pentonville Road
London
N1 9LZ
Tel: 0171 833 2181 for details of your nearest branch

NATIONAL YOUTH FOUNDATION
P.O. Box 606
Carlingford
New South Wales
2118
Australia
Tel: 00 612 211 1788

NATIONAL CHILDREN'S CENTRE
Brian Jackson Centre
New North Parade
Huddersfield
HD1 5JP
Tel: 0484519988

MINISTRY OF YOUTH
P.O. Box 10-300
Wellington
New Zealand
Tel: 00 644 471 2158

ANTI-BULLYING CAMPAIGN (ABC)
10 Borough High Street
London
SE1 9QQ
Tel: 0171 378 1446

CHILDREN'S PROTECTION SOCIETY, AUSTRALIA
Tel: 010 613 458 3566

Index

Photocredits

All the pictures in this book are by Roger Vlitos, apart from page 13, top left; Frank Spooner. The publishers wish to acknowledge that all the people photographed in this book are models.